Everything You Always Wanted to Know About Cemeteries… But Were Afraid to Ask!!

By D. Weathers-Lee

TABLE OF CONTENTS

INTRODUCTION

Having been an advisor to cemetery families for over 15 years, I discovered that many people have a fear of cemeteries. American society has indeed encouraged mystery surrounding the hard-working, dedicated caretakers in this industry.

Many of the questions that have been asked over the years are being discussed in this book. My belief is that education will result in a healthier opinion about the most unpopular subject in the world.

Please do not interpret my light portrayal as any deliberate lack of compassion or disrespect to the memories of any of

our loved ones. It seems that people are usually more comfortable with accepting this information in a lighter, kinder mode.

DEDICATION

Over the years I've thought of my gratitude to my sophomore speech teacher, Ms. P. She encouraged me to never stop writing. My late parents have been a bright guiding light through my life. I want to thank my supportive husband, children, grandchildren and grands for their love that motivates me to teach and share information with others.

To all the wonderful associates in the industry who have shared their wisdom, I am grateful. Sincere thanks to the hundreds of people who have shared those precious moments of their lives. Their experiences have encouraged me to share some of the lessons that, I have learned from them.

My goal is that you gain support from the
information presented in the pages ahead; and
that this book becomes a useful reference guide.

Sincerely,
Deborah Weathers-Lee
Funeral and Cemetery Pre-Planning Consultant

Everything You Always Wanted to Know

About Cemeteries But, Were Afraid to Ask!

Showmen's Rest

Woodlawn Memorial Park   Forest Park, Illinois

To my dear, brave cemetery people who hesitantly wander into local cemetery offices across the country, now that you've gotten your courage to come by and ask a few questions....... You can be certain of one thing; you need to begin asking questions about a difficult task.

The cemetery counselors are there for your protection. These wonderful caretakers are attempting to kindly inform you of what you are approaching, eventually in your life; as if you didn't know. These workers aren't trying to just sell you something. Education, experience, skills and compassion are utilized by them; to help you and help your family from the realities that will surface later, some of which will leave lasting scars on family relationships. Remember; your expressions of apprehension and fear are what you are teaching your children and grandchildren. We should not teach them to be fearful of what is an inevitable part of every life. We should instead teach them the importance of knowledge and understanding about our end of life. Teach them to live good lives, respect life and leave a positive legacy for future generations to be proud of.

Why You Pre-Plan?

Well, one of the big reasons that you should buy ahead of time is because you need to buy so much.

What I mean is that it seems to be a simple purchase. However, selecting and purchasing cemetery property is quite a complicated process. The reason is probably due to the individual options that exist. Everyone has his or her own idea of what should or should not take place at the time of death. Therefore, it involves numerous steps of decision making, detailed planning and numerous bills. The prices are quietly increasing each year in this industry.

If you continue to postpone seeking information; your decision may become a huge financial mistake, one you will always regret.

Give yourself the opportunity to make clear and wise decisions before it becomes a mandatory task. I want to emphasize that you need to start seeking this information while you are young; don't make the mistake of thinking that this subject applies only to the elderly.

You should at least learn what services, merchandise,

and fees you will need to pay for. Ask about the types

of plans that are offered. Many cemeteries offer some type of pre-payment plan.

Some cemeteries today are also offering full-service funeral pre-payment plans. (If they do; usually they have some affiliation to a funeral home). It is no longer necessary for you to wait until a death occurs before you begin shopping. They are usually secured by life insurance protection. In my opinion, life insurance funded funeral plans are the safest investment. Your prices are protected against future inflation. Go in and ask if your cemetery offers these plans;

and how they work. Take a seat and open your eyes and your mind. Honestly, you can use some valid information for yourself, whether you believe it or not.

I believe that we should never stop learning until the day we die. It's very true that knowledge gained from learning helps to empower you. Please don't live the rest of your life in denial. Life can be so peaceful and worry free for you, if you just prepare for the inevitable. We will all stop by deaths door; one day. When that day will come, who knows? Tomorrow is never promised to any of us. The one thing we know for sure.... we must all have our last day.

Pre-Planning Says, "I Love You"

It makes no sense; that you are wondering about all these very important things, but you remain afraid to go seek out the answers; that you know, you want to know. Why are you afraid to find out the facts about one of the most important parts of your life? What could be more important than the end of your life? It's your life! You run around planning and planning for every other event in your life.

We enjoy our lives so much that we don't want to think about it ending.

The thought of life ending is just so frightening. I agree; but we are not being fair to ourselves and our loved ones when we don't help them with some of these huge tasks.

Planning is only saying family and friends I really love you. I love you so much that I don't want to cause you any additional pain and suffering when I die. I want to share this experience with you while I am healthy and in my right mind.

I want to show you how courageous I am and teach you how to be that way.

I don't want this to be a troubling chore if I am lying ill or weak. That would be very wrong for me to put you through so much pain and suffering. That's a big amount of pressure for you to bear. Please take my advice and go in and talk to the cemetery people.

They are waiting to meet you and help you. They won't bite! They will help you save some money and prevent some agony.

So, if you have been avoiding this dismal thought about cemeteries, graves, caskets, headstones, and much, much more; please get off the couch.

Please quit speeding past the cemetery. Don't cover your ears and eyes when someone mentions us. Quit announcing to your family that you are not ready to talk about it. Get with it! Get your house in order!

The Conversation

One of the most difficult things for us to think about is the future death of our parents. I know that children are very shy of talking about a subject of this nature; no matter how old we are it is very awkward. Sometimes you are busy with careers, children and mates; and you tend to postpone those important talks with your senior aged parents or others close to you.

 Maybe another family member will take over that part and get you out of that awkward place permanently; maybe not. Suppose you have tried to bring up the subject and are denied entry into that zone. Maybe your parents have tried to mention it with confusion and uncertainty. Maybe, instead of engaging them in more conversation about the root of their uncertainty, you postpone that important opportunity to get some solid facts realized.

Here's one practice that I believe will help. No matter the situation; when your parents get to age 65; it becomes necessary for you to become a close companion to them. It is now time for you to snoop about their affairs; I mean about everything. It becomes time for the conversation to start happening, if it hasn't occurred yet. Find out what insurance they have purchased; see the policies with your eyes. Call the insurance companies and request current status information.

Never go away with some nice verbal information only. Verify, Verify, Verify! Make sure that the budget is working, and the bills are getting paid on time. Sometimes cemetery property is owned or inherited. Never assume that everything has been taken care of. This presents the perfect opportunity to schedule an appointment to visit the cemetery office to review the files together.

Verify, Verify, Verify! Sometimes funeral plans or cremation plans have been pre-paid. Look for documents stating this and call the funeral or cremation service provider and confirm the information.

Verify, Verify, Verify!

If you don't find any proof through documents. You need to take notes; and start creating a plan to get started on all the things that should have been done but are not. Becoming well organized now will be a big reward later. Establish a location or company to fulfill the plan and start to ask all of the essential questions needed about services.

Silly Question?
No Such Thing!

Structure a payment plan that will work well with your budget allowance. Why not?

That is my most frequent question to you. Why not? Don't you realize that one of these days you will need a burial place, you will need to pay for cemetery fees, and you will also need to pay necessary funeral expenses? Don't you understand that you will be meeting with a funeral director one day? Yes you; either alive; standing with your eyes wide open, asking many questions or quietly lying dead with your eyes shut. Why not? Remember, how you told your children as they were growing up to not be afraid and not to be worried? Speaking to strangers about uncomfortable subjects is quite a challenge, I agree. You must teach yourselves to be brave.

Cemetery counselors have never heard a silly question before. Funeral Home directors have never heard a foolish question. People always seem to feel very awkward about their curiosity. They seem to feel that their thoughts border on the ridiculous.

Don't feel that way; we have all had those moments. That's the way that we learn. I have noticed that a great percentage of your information grows from myths and rumors. It's a great idea to find out the truth and set the records straight.

Find a cemetery that appeals to you, usually the visual experience must be good. Maybe you would prefer to look at the cemetery that your family has always used.

Cemeteries usually offer easy time payment plans for your convenience. This is the big advantage for shopping

 pre-need, (well ahead of time, for use). Make sure that your cemetery has the endowment care fund,

(ECF) included in your purchase price. This will offer you future years of general maintenance at no cost to the family. You will never be billed for the upkeep of the lawns, trimming of trees and adjustments of the memorials or other serviceable care.

It's very important that you go into the establishment that you are curious about and bring your list of questions, which seem to stick in your mind. Information is power.

Have It Your Way

Ask for a professional and knowledgeable person to please provide you with some time to get some facts straight.

Remember, the temperament and personality of the staff, should be something tolerable for you. If you have some positive signals, please apologize for not scheduling an appointment. Ask if another day would be more convenient. Please exchange information and keep your appointment or please call if you must reschedule.

The people doing this job are serious professionals and they deserve a great amount of respect for their consulting time. If you don't feel comfortable with this approach, think about calling in or writing a letter to receive information a little more indirectly. At any rate, remember, you're never under any obligation and you only owe it to yourself and your surviving family and friends, who become responsible after you have departed this life.

Remember, this is the Big Hallelujah that you're seeking information about. Find out how many options are possible to celebrate your final walk up the stairway to heaven.

It's important to really do it your way. Don't expect other people to try to figure out what that means. You hold, all that vital information. Will you please start writing down some of that stuff?

You know the little things that are so important and so special for you. You know the way you part your hair exactly 3" above your ear lobe on the left. You know you really would rather not wear your eyeglasses. Your favorite song, they may not be sure; you loved several songs. You always loved a special poem that was read at your high school graduation. How are they supposed to know that?

You know that special dress that you look especially great wearing; and you secretly would like it kept in a special place. Do you want a golf club in your casket? Remember those special passages in your Bible that you have always loved, should they be read at your funeral?

 And don't forget you want your 1965 Red Ford Mustang, to be parked at the door of funeral home and then driven by your grandsons behind the hearse to the cemetery.

You can really do it your way; by helping your family to know just what to do. Let your family know just what your wishes are.

What Do You Really Want?

Do you know how special the smell of cookie dough is to your children? The aroma of fresh baked cookies during your visitation would make them feel so much peace and love.

 Find out if your wildest wishes are possible. Can I really have a lake front memorial service? Is it possible to be cremated and have my ashes divided into 5 containers for my husband and my 4 children? Can I wear my favorite pink crystal brooch on my dress? Should I have to show my grey hair?

 My husband says he would rather wear his suit and tie during his wake; but as soon as it ends, please allow him to change into something more comfortable for his burial. Is this normal? Can my family please play some of my favorite lively music at my visitation?

My husband wants to be cremated and nothing else. He says don't waste any money on all that stuff; do I still need a funeral director or funeral home? Should I be ready to share my plans with my family? Do they need to help me with my arrangements?

Suppose my kids say, mom you are really bothering me with all this talk about pre-planning? Does this mean that maybe I should stop all this planning and make them happy and just do nothing? By the looks of all the possibilities that can surface; I would say you don't want your children stuck with the overwhelming decisions, that you see can come into the picture.

It's a very sound idea to start to at least make your wishes known by writing them down. Some cemeteries have personal organizer books for the purpose of recording all your information and your wishes. This can be very helpful to your family; provided you don't go hiding all your notes, where no one would ever find them until long after they really need them.

This may help you to realize that your family needs to be included in knowing what your wishes are. This may also be the start of really helping you to plan those much-needed conversations about all the important details that you need to share with one another. Personalization is the key here. What are your real wishes? Survivors matter so much. Keep them informed. What do you really want? Have it your way!

Is The Casket Included?

This scenario has happened on several occasions, for example, people instinctively will ask; "How much does it cost for a burial these days?" I begin by stating, first you must purchase your grave. Next, I explain the need for an interment fee, which is the cost for our cemetery grounds men to open the grave for the upcoming burial. You must purchase a grave liner or a vault. There are other tasks that are completed including sometimes assembling a tent, installing a burial vault or preparing the cemetery chapel. The cosmetic appearance of the area is enhanced by green turf carpets, and family chairs facing the grave site. The casket must be lowered, the vault cover set, the grave is closed and filled with fresh dirt. The headstone or monument is reset either at the site or will be on order.

All the above are subject to charges including the burial site, merchandise, services, tax, and fees. The total can be around $5000 and up. Some of these people will inevitably look at me and ask; "And, is the casket included?" No! The casket is not included! The prices today are much more than years ago, so many are greatly surprised. The funeral home will be providing the casket along with their other services and merchandise.

Many people don't see a difference between the cemetery and the funeral home. We are two distinctively separate entities of our industry; even when they seem to be combined in their locations. The reason for this great big grey area is that most people would rather not become actively involved; this is a mistake.

Another factor is that many families, at the time of a death may not be required to go the cemetery office. The funeral director seems to oversee everything; however, 99% of the time he or she fulfills these things as a courtesy and as a means of controlling cost.

I feel 100% that whenever physically possible; you still should follow up with the cemetery directly. If possible, you should go to the cemetery in person. I find it concerning to discover people who never see a grave location until the moment they arrive at the cemetery for the burial. It is truly a disservice to anyone who has experienced this. It's just a good idea to see the cemetery site ahead of time. The family may prefer to inspect the site and the surrounding area.

 Become aware; in case changes of location or cosmetic improvements are needed before the funeral procession arrives.

In recent years, some cases have surfaced regarding the abuse of human remains and the misuse of caskets and burial vaults. Laws, regulations, and ethics of companies with high standards and the practice of quality service, would never permit such crimes to occur to their client families and their loved ones.

So contrary to rumors; the bad people in this industry are few and far between. Cemeteries are extremely careful and respectful of managing the care of your loved ones when they arrive for their stay.

The industry is highly regulated in most states in the US. Severe penalties are guaranteed for those breaking any of the laws.

Chicagocooperatorsnews.com

Books and graduate cap by Fotolio2013

Become Educated Consumers

I'm here today calling on all people of age 21 to 65, begin to act more responsibly about your destination. I can educate you and you can pass the information on to your families and friends. It's not a very popular job but, we all must do it one day.

Someday you all will be called upon directly or indirectly to help with some detail, opinion or advice of a funeral, burial, cremation or other, of a loved one. I want all of you to become educated consumers. This is the area that is extremely important to be smart about.

Remember knowledge will empower you. Pre-plan for yourself and encourage your loved ones to do the same. They will always appreciate your wisdom.

The last decade has really shown a great consistent increase of the people that are getting involved in pre-planning. They have learned and become wiser by observing the wisdom of others. They have witnessed the peace of mind that those families have. They have seen the financial picture not disrupted or shattered by sudden unexpected expenses. Some of our leading polls show that pre-need shoppers are on the rise.

Get Your House in Order

You're never too young, to start purchasing for yourself and your spouse if applicable, your parents, and even your children. Why are you waiting for your children to take care of everything for you? You have always taken care of everything yourself. Why the sudden change? Are you really waiting for someone else to take care of your final business? Or are you just a little worried about how to go about this. Maybe you aren't sure you have quite enough courage to step in or call in, to ask a few important questions.

I have a suggestion for those of you who have children.... sit down and gather the courage to have that conversation with them. I guarantee it will probably be the most awkward, uncomfortable and frightening experience you've ever had. It may not go smoothly either. If you've never in your life talked about this sort of thing with your family; don't expect that it will be welcomed. It is very normal to sometimes get quite a negative backlash. Quite frankly, kids never want that picture in their head; of you deceased. It's a sad, depressing, and frightening thought. On the other hand, they may have been afraid to bring up the subject and become so relieved that you did decide to talk. If there are no children to discuss your final life information with; then a spouse, relative, or friend will have to be your audience. If there is no family or friends; please seek professional assistance. I think that you may not want to ever face the reality of aging, but you need to know that our life ends someday. When that day arrives, a cemetery plan and a funeral plan needs to have been put into place. This plan should be documented from start to finish. This plan should include as much detail as possible and preferably this plan should be funded. If the plan has not been funded; it should have accessible funding, or insurance benefits easily available for the next of kin or legal representative. When matters become complicated, do not hesitate to seek consultation from a legal professional.

This conversation is so serious it should be discussed early in adult life and not avoided until old age sets in. The family needs to get comfortable with such conversations and I think, the earlier in life the better. Then the reality of the circumstances is a lot easier to understand and less intimidating. Our greatest responsibility before death is to get our house in order. The sooner you begin to organize and implement your tasks; the better off you are, and your loved ones.

What's The Opening & Closing?

The easy way to remember what the **opening and closing** means is to realize that every person that is brought to the cemetery is placed inside of some type of space. The spaces all must be opened for them to enter and then finally they need to be closed. This procedure is far more detailed than that, however; it gives you more of an idea about the terms being used to describe it. The professional service term for ground burial of a person in a casket or a person in an urn, is called **interment.** The professional service term for a person entering a mausoleum crypt space in a casket is an **entombment.** The service term for an urn (a container for cremated remains) entering a niche space, in a mausoleum or columbarium; (an independent niche bank with multiple spaces); is called **inurnment.** If inurned ashes will have a ground burial, it is also called an inurnment. So, in comparison to the technical terms, it's so much easier to say the **opening and closing**. Also remember that every cemetery usually charges for every single item of merchandise and for every delivery of service, fees are usually charged. Fees can also be prepaid years in advance. Some companies operate like others but, I don't think any are operating exactly alike.

 Remember every cemetery has its rules and regulations. Respect the rules; your experiences will be much less stressful. Be aware of what they are in advance, so you won't be disappointed later. Keep in mind that those rules and regulations were applied for a reason. As a property owner, you will eventually appreciate having them. Rules and regulations are enforced to protect you.

What Is A Burial Vault?

In 1880; Leo Haase, developed an outer burial container made from bricks. By the 1960's; most cemeteries realized that in order to avoid a very bad maintenance nightmare, the use of concrete outer burial containers, was to become a required product for each burial.

 During earlier years other types of containers were permitted such as burial bags, caskets, and wooden boxes. These burials proved to create uneven areas that affected the level placement of memorials and potential cave in conditions. This made the appearance in these areas look very poor. These areas also became quite treacherous for visitors to walk out to seek their loved ones. Most cemeteries today will require the use of at least a standard concrete outer burial container.

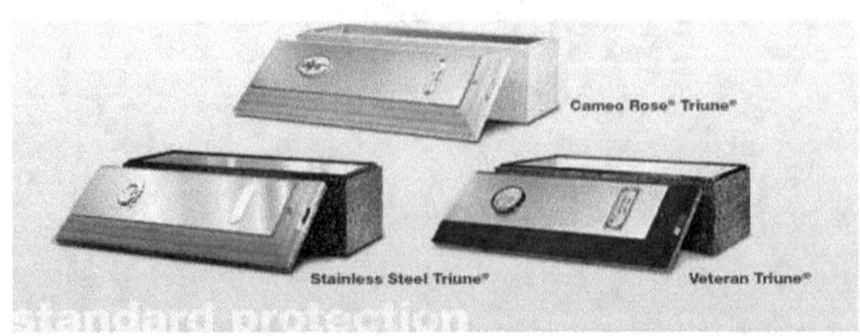

The minimal priced concrete containers do meet the requirements of the cemetery. Remember, the minimal priced container also called grave liners or grave boxes are not built as solidly as are the vaults. They do not offer a sealing lid. This can make a difference to the amount of protection provided from the weight of the earth, large tree roots, and the underground elements. They may often have drainage holes in the floor of the base.

Burial vaults are priced slightly higher but are better containers. The lids of the vaults are built with a special asphalt sealant installed in the grooves of the lid. It activates when the tongue in groove cover is placed on to the base. This is done usually after the casket is lowered into the grave and into the base of the burial vault. Burial vaults are starting at 2000 lbs. of concrete and sometimes reinforced steel.

Vault companies offer whatever comfort level of cost that your pocket can stand. They offer painted covers that match or coordinate with the color of the casket. They are personalized with nameplates that show the name of the deceased and their year of birth and death. Emblems in various designs are offered to enhance the covers. The linings and covers can be upgraded to offer vinyl, plastic products, stainless steel, simulated marble, copper or bronze.

The usage of these strong containers also assures us that, the heavy weight of the earth and any possibility of trucks passing over; will not cause any damage below ground.

Your choice depends on how you feel about that. I have met people who could not feel comfortable with their decision if the vault weren't extremely weighted with layers of linings.

There are others who simply make no bones about it and request to use the least expensive container possible. If you are in doubt, a middle-priced vault may be a safe selection. Burial vaults have indeed become a big business. There are even burial vaults with customized artwork, photographs, and artistic personalization on them. There are a lot of vault options out there.

However, at some point, it becomes your personal decision of what you feel is best for your loved one and for yourself.

Cemeteries would look like sections of pedestrian potholes and worst without the use of these containers.
Not to mention the danger we would be in while trying to visit the cemetery. Burial vaults make your visiting experience much safer.

 Burial vaults also give families the comfort of knowing that their loved one is safe in his or her final resting place.

Meaningful Memorials

Every life has a story to tell. Memorialization helps to leave a visual tribute in honor of the life lived and an enduring symbol of love and family heritage. Every person buried in the cemetery does not have a memorial. When we lose someone dear to us, we try to keep them alive in our hearts. That is why memorials are so important.

Flush or flat memorials are very beautiful when you are standing over them. The problem is you can usually only see them when you are standing over them.

Monuments are tall and wide and can be seen from a distance. This makes it much easier to locate your family burial property. I would advise you to ask what type of memorial is allowed, when selecting your burial sites. Not checking in advance can be extremely disappointing later.

A common question that people will ask is, about the proper waiting time before you can install a memorial after a burial. Unless it is a cultural or religious custom; there is no wait time needed to get started.

Each family can create a memorial that truly reflects the unique qualities of the individual and honors their lives in a meaningful way. Each cemetery has their own special schedules for ordering and installation. Check with your cemetery office guidelines on the park rules for memorial sizes, material, etc.

Personalization is important; remember memorials can be as individual as the people they honor. Give yourself the freedom of expression to tell their stories in meaningful ways. Memorials can attest faith and include laser scenes and portraits.

Bronze emblems or engraving can symbolize important hobbies, careers, music, organizations, military affiliation, dance, ceramic photos, carved flower beds, art, and much more. Sometimes they are filled with letters of love and beautiful poetry. They also make a great canvas for photo montages. A photo life story is quite a remarkable expression of love and devotion.

A memorial that is crafted out of love and caring shall forever say, "You will never be forgotten." The cemetery is usually able to assist you with your designing process.

*Memorial Center; Palms Gardens, Las Vegas, NV

Personalize Your Final Resting Place

Granite is the rock most often quarried as a "Dimension stone" (a natural rock material that has been cut into blocks or slabs of specific length, width and thickness). Granite is hard enough to resist most abrasion, strong enough to bear significant weight, inert enough to resist weathering and it accepts a brilliant polish. These characteristics make it very desirable and useful.

 Granite has been used for thousands of years for cemetery memorials of many styles. Rough-cut and polished granite is used in buildings, bridges, paving, monuments and many other exterior projects. Indoors and outdoors, polished granite slabs and tiles are used in mausoleum buildings.

Granite is frequently selected because it is a prestige material, used in projects to produce impressions of elegance, durability, and lasting quality. Most of the granite produced in the United States comes from high quality deposits in five states: Massachusetts, Georgia, New Hampshire, South Dakota and Idaho. (http://geology.com)

Graceland Estate Memphis, Tennessee Elvis Presley Family Bronze Memorial

Bronze was made before 3000 BC. It is the oldest and the strongest metal known to man. Bronze is strengthened by the combination of copper and tin. **It** is used in many areas but especially in the cemeteries for headstones. Bronze today has been perfected in its finished and aging quality. Bronze now is available in various textures and shades of green, blue, black, classic brown and red.

Bronze can provide illustrated photo images and sculpted images with meaningful wording. Memorials of this type many times are selected, designed and installed in advance of need. Some people find this detail strange or weird. I admire their choice to be pro-active, and I think it is a very wise decision. The owners are proud of their creations and are guaranteed to never be without their memorial tribute.

US Veteran Bronze Headstone on Granite Base
*(base sold by the non-government cemetery)

U.S. Veterans (Non-Service-Related Death) The U.S. government offers a burial allowance of up to $700.00 for some veterans that are buried in private cemeteries. The next of kin or claimant may be reimbursed within VA guidelines.

VA Form 21-530/ Application for Burial Benefits

*Check V.A. or local cemetery for details and

The government provides the American veteran with the option of having a bronze headstone, granite headstone, or marble (marble, not recommended in colder climates); made for their grave site at private cemeteries. They make a proud and dignified tribute to the military service endeavors of each veteran. The veteran must have had an honorable discharge from the military.

The headstone can be ordered by your cemetery counselor by submitting the Record & Report of Separation, if the veteran served before 1951. If after 1951, then the family will need to provide the DD-214, Honorable Discharge papers.

Veterans are given burials at US National Cemeteries at no cost. The spouse or surviving spouse, minor child, & some unmarried adult children (special guidelines are applicable), may also be buried in a national cemetery, even if that veteran is not buried or memorialized in a national cemetery.

The VA does not make funeral arrangements or perform cremations. Families should make these arrangements with a funeral home or cremation service. The funeral or cremation will be at the family's expense.

The details are available at Veteran Affairs Department website http://www.va.gov.

Personalize Your Funeral

Most American funeral services in 2013 are still set up the same as they were at the funeral of Abraham Lincoln, in 1865. There are more standard and conservative services in the Midwest than in the rest of the nation.

Funerals in the south are a jubilant journey to heaven event. The joy is so vibrant you can almost see the band of angels in chariots, waiting in the front of the church. Funerals in California are video and web cam events, with pre-taped video message narratives on wide screens, with the deceased speaking to all in attendance. Some funerals are musical extravaganzas with live bands and singers.

I saw a family that had a poker night visitation; and a jazz musicians' quartet soothing the soul of those attending his memorial.

What I'm trying to say is; it is important to personalize your special day in a special way. Many people have begun to find the joy of creating a very respectful service that personalizes and highlights the attributes of their loved one.

 Funeral services have become more of a celebration of the life that was lived by our deceased loved ones.

I don't mean to sound as if I am not respectful of the sorrow and pain that is being felt by so many during this time. However, many people say, they felt their ability to cope was strengthened by the method of the tribute. They felt relieved and joyous that the souls of those they mourn are gone on to a better existence.

One thing that is very true; the death of a loved one is universal and is the single most horrific event in our lives.

Everything changes and will never be the same again. It is our recovery process that matters so much.

The pain can be so overwhelming that we don't want to face that raw truth again but somehow; we must learn to get through it. When support from family and friends are no longer immediately at our side, we must learn to wear the tough skin. We then eventually, learn to live on.

Mausoleums

Interior Community Mausoleum

Mausoleums are final resting places built above the ground. Caskets placed into mausoleum spaces are not required to have burial vaults. The caskets are placed into casket sized chambers that are built into the walls of the structure. Each chamber is called a mausoleum crypt. A ventilation source cycles throughout the crypt day and night. Each chamber provides a clean and dry area for the caskets to remain.

Some of the crypts are single sites and some are for companions to rest together. The caskets are sealed inside of the crypts by several layers of large marble or granite covers. The names of the deceased are placed on the covers either by a bronze nameplate, bronze lettering, or engraving.

Mausoleums are the oldest form of resting place. The ancient pyramids of Egypt were used to rest the bodies of the pharaohs and their families. Jesus Christ was laid to rest inside of a garden tomb in Jerusalem.

Community mausoleums are built for multiple families to share the cost as they share the building. Many families have discovered that the cost of purchasing these types of mausoleum space, are more economical than they had ever realized. They are usually quite comparable in cost to ground burial.

Some crypts are outdoors with lovely garden settings and others are indoors with beautiful and peaceful surroundings. Some are built below ground. These are called lawn crypt gardens.

Private mausoleums are popular for single families, faith groups, savings clubs, and others that have larger budgets to have buildings constructed. These projects usually take several months to select the proper location and design. Private estates are available from one single unit up to accommodations for 12 or more family members.

Landscaping, benches, vases, custom hardware, stained glass windows, bronze doors, prayer alters, etc., can be added to beautify and personalize each building.

Overall, families who do select mausoleum for their loved ones are very satisfied. They enjoy the peace and serenity of the entombment service and feel very confident that their loved ones are comfortably resting in a clean and dry environment.

All of you who have always been curious about mausoleum please try visiting some of them in your area. If you find a mausoleum that you like; just stop by the office and ask about availability and pricing. Try touring several and compare prices and features. Share your discovery with your family; see if you can find a touring companion who may be interested in learning some vital facts with you.

Cremation Options

Cremation is trending and becoming the choice of many more people than ever before. Cost is a big reason for this spike of cremation services.

Growing popularity; however, has caused price increases for cremation. Cremation is the process of burning a human dead body approximately 4-5 hours, until it becomes brittle, dried, calcified bones, which are then pulverized to appear like ashes.

Cremation has a great benefit which allows the family time after the process has been completed; to decide about memorial services and destination.

The cremation urn can go home and be placed on the mantle. But what about the other people who might want to visit and pay their respects?

Do they need to get a visitors pass for your home? Will your ashes move from room to room and maybe end up in the closet or in the basement? Or will you follow some of the unusual final request of dumping, throwing, and scattering ashes almost anywhere you can imagine.

I feel that the best solution is a proper final resting place in a cemetery. It may be an expense that you wish you could avoid; but I think that too many of us are saving a bundle of money and losing the opportunity to have that emotional connection time and time again. This is only possible to achieve if you select the options available at a cemetery.

This will officially document your end of life and assign your final resting place. Cremation does present many options, but we must make careful decisions.

It is important to fulfill the wishes of our loved ones; however, we must be aware of our survivors and the legacy we want to leave behind.

One of those options could be burial in a cremation garden in a small grave with a memorial installed on top of it. You may arrange a burial to share a grave with another family member. Couples who have chosen cremation may want to share a standard burial space or be buried simultaneously. Cremation burial urns may require a cremation vault as seen in the previous image.

Others may want to have a modest niche with a personalized name plate. Still there is the glass front niche, which can be personalized to show a beautiful urn, flowers and photos, and special keepsakes.
Some cemeteries have niche columbarium space indoors and outdoors.

There are also granite cremation benches, and customized monument vases, bronze headstones with cremation receptacles, cremation boulders, cremation diamonds, keepsake urns (miniature size), jewelry, and much more.

Remember, our lives on earth have had many distinct meanings to our survivors. Our future generations do inevitably search for us. We never are always knowledgeable of the personal impact that, we have on others. Our final resting place is important to many in our lives.

If you are a person who has already purchased your cemetery property, I think that it's a good idea to call or visit the cemetery and update your records. This is a good time to review what kind of expenses are still ahead of you. It's a really good idea to set up a plan for payment or pay the charges in full.

It just really makes good sense. You'll be helping the family that loves you so much and vice versa. You'll be saving a bundle of money (in the long run). The best part is, knowing that you have completed that important obligation you owe to yourself and your loved ones.

You will finally realize what true peace of mind means; in knowing you have done all the right things for the right reasons.

Memorial Services

When cremation is your choice for final disposition, memorial services can be very beautiful events. The family can express love in unique and personal ways. Cremation can allow the family time for personal ceremonies.

There is no immediate need to rush for preparation of services unless that is your preference.

Family planning can include photo displays, videos, favorite music, singing, personal belongings such as, favorite T-shirts, musical instruments, hats, vehicles, hobby displays, favorite snacks, refreshments, etc.

Some locations for memorial services can be as unique as you can imagine. Ideas such as inside of chapels, parks, cemeteries, scenic locations, aboard boats, restaurants, and more are utilized for these special memorial plans. Special they really are! I've attended several and they are very upbeat events for all who attend. Guest usually participate in some way by creating readings, sharing stories, songs, etc.

The atmosphere is very inspirational and very positive. The sounds of love, joy and peace resonate throughout. Those in attendance usually leave with a feeling of positive remembrance of their loved one. Peace of mind is sure to follow you home.

Don't hesitate to plan memorial services your way. Family members don't always agree with your decision for cremation of your loved one. Don't let that stop your planning for a very special day thoughtfully prepared for your loved one.

 So, if cremation is your personal choice. Plan in a way that will leave your family happy about your decision for cremation. I'm sure everyone involved will be pleased.

THE GUARDIAN.COM

DECISIONS!

DECISIONS!

SO MANY DECISIONS?

Can I Change My Original Plans?

What if your decision regarding final disposition is troublesome to you, after you leave the cemetery? You're only human. As you know we can really struggle over tough decisions. I have found that sometimes people will express their desire to change from the choices that were originally made for destination of their loved one. This is not very common, but it does happen. There are many reasons for concerns to enter the picture.

Maybe you have relocated to another part of the country and would like to bring your loved one to your new area. Visiting will be more convenient. You may in fact feel more peace being closer. Perhaps you have been contemplating mausoleum and no longer want your loved one in a ground burial location.

There may be a more desirable area within the same cemetery that you like much better than the original selection. Reasons are your personal ideas and your personal choice. I have always considered it helpful to discuss the possibility cautiously. All situations are very different and very detailed with many legalities.

There are always many facts that must be considered first, such as the burial rights, who is the owner of the specific burial rights of the site being considered? Who is the legal next of kin of the decedent? Is that person or persons, parents, spouse, adult children, or other? Are they in agreement with your decision? How long has it been since the death occurred? If ground burial was selected for the final disposition, what type of vault or burial container was used at the time of burial? Historical details are very important to discover before pursuing the matter any further.

Disinterment is the process by which a dead body is legally exhumed from its final resting place...................... If there are no legal complications, however, the body can be legally exhumed without the fear of accusations that a gravesite has been defiled.

When you bury your loved ones, most of the time you do so with the intent that they remain where they are buried forever. However, sometimes circumstances arise where it becomes necessary to disturb our loved one's final resting place, and remove them from their grave, at least for a time.

Disinterment's are more common than you think. These services are provided for personal satisfaction as well as unusual circumstances.

With the assistance of experienced professionals, funeral directors, authorizations, legal document filing, etc. your request can be fulfilled. You can have a successful relocation of your loved one and a more peaceful state of mind about your decision.

Many people have a difficult time accepting the idea of relocating a loved one. I believe that most people that inquire about the possibilities are determined to follow through at some point.

Disinterment is not complimentary. This detailed measure will be costly. If you decide to begin the process, start gathering details with a knowledgeable cemetery professional. The best way to organize your plan without losing the farm is to preplan.

The way to preplan is to begin your financial commitment with purchasing your new preferred location in advance. You will need to purchase an interment fee (opening & closing fee) . You may be advised about a new vault purchase or even casket in some situations. Every situation is unique.

Even if its years away, it makes financial sense to investigate what kind of preplanning programs your cemetery has to offer. Inquire about sales or specials, if any at the cemetery. This doesn't get you instant results but will allow you to reach your goals more comfortably later.

The price of peace of mind doesn't compare to the cost of living a life with inner sadness and regret. Purchasing at today's prices in order to experience savings later is a wise way to go.

Grief Is Love

Family relationships are so important and so very complex, especially when a family member or friend passes away. Grief causes great amounts of pain. I am always so thankful to discover that love never dies, long after our loved ones have departed; love still lives.

Families experiencing turmoil at the time of loss are very concerning to me. Emotions are raw. Stress levels are at their peak and feelings can be hurt for years to come. Relationships among family members can be shattered.

From the writings of Jennifer Williamson, I found much comfort and truth. Please let me share her words:

"It hurts because it mattered, and it will always matter. I've learned that grief is another name for **Love** and no matter how deep, your grief makes a home in you, love will always leave a window open. A window for fresh air in the middle of the storm, for hope that comes after you've lost all hope.

There is an invisible thread connecting you heart to all hearts, you to all life. Grief is a heavy weight to carry and it's also an anchor in love. It's not something you can rush or push past. It's feels so like fear that it's hard to see how it can leave room for love.

But Love finds its way through you. You learn to breathe it in and out, the love and the fear, all at the same time. You'll find pain in letting go and hope in what you pick up. This, because you're here to experience it all."

The need to get in touch with your feelings is needed on a regular basis. If you're having an extremely difficult time after the death of a loved one, and more than 6 months has passed by; and you're still feeling very down and out. Please talk to someone, seeking professional help is sometimes very beneficial. I urge you to speak to someone about what you're going through. There are grief support groups available, private counseling, grief hotlines, friends, clergy, etc.

Please remember without love there could not be room for grief.

DENIAL
ANGER
BARGAINING
DEPRESSION
ACCEPTANCE

Visiting?

Visiting the cemetery is a means of showing respect to the memory of our loved ones. Many people visit the gravesites and place flowers and personal decorations. Some find it comforting tending to the care and beauty of the site soon after the burial takes place. This is also helpful with locating the site easier, especially if there is no headstone at the grave. Getting lost in the cemetery can be very frustrating and upsetting.

I personally find that visiting the cemetery is very therapeutic. I go to my parents' graves and have long conversations. I keep them up to date with my life. I have learned to share with them all the things that they have missed over the years. It wasn't always easy to do that. Flushing my tear ducts and purging the blues has a way of healing the mind, body and soul. Visiting your loved one's grave gives you permission to grieve. You gain a better perspective of your life.

You begin to better understand, the days following the worst day of your life. Visiting the cemetery helps us to strengthen our power and endurance to learn, how to cope with our loss and gradually move our lives forward again.

Please feel free to visit the gravesite, crypt or niche of the person you love. Remember, when you love someone unconditionally; your love continues and on even after their death. Visiting allows an emotional void to be filled, and that connection is very healthy.

Don't forget to check the visitors' rules and regulations of the cemetery. Visit alone or with someone; stay a few moments or relax for a while. You may sit in your car, bring a chair or lay on the grass.

If occasional visits don't seem to be your thing; maybe, you'll do better to start out with a special birthday or anniversary visit. Maybe your family will be interested in making an annual plan to meet at the site. Encourage the younger family members to participate even if you may not be feeling this interest. Let them know that it's okay to do this. The benefits are numerous for the mental and emotional well-being of your family and the stability of your family heritage.

Family Heritage

Cemeteries are like peace and love centers. You can go for walks or do a little jogging. You can sit a while and get in touch with nature. You can reflect upon precious memories, meditate, pray, gather your thoughts, sing or even scream your feelings out loud.

Feel free to bring a sandwich and read a book.

Visit with someone you love and those you once knew. Learn plenty about history.

Cemeteries hold the mysteries of millions of lives, and their contributions to thousands of years of history.

I am constantly amazed by the amount of interest that exists for information about genealogy. More than we realize there are a huge amount of people who are searching for their family heritage.

Lets' do not permit our fears to create the ripple effect upon our future generations. The information has gotten lost over time for many reasons, however; generations of people look at the cemetery to solve some of their problems. Family history is based on finding one clue at a time and then finding facts to support them. Many of those clues can sometimes be found in the cemetery.

The branches of family trees and puzzle pieces of history hide underneath each headstone.

Genealogy is fueled by the existence of these magnificent parks full of our numerous footprints that have been left here on this earth. Don't fear them; get engaged. It's never too late

to start ,.........or should I say, don't wait too late to start!

Keep in mind; cemeteries are also places for the living.

NATIONAL GEOGRAPHIC
Find more wallpapers at www.nationalgeographic.com
© 2006 National Geographic Society. All rights reserved.
Photograph by Bob Sacha

JAMES H.
RICHARDS
1954   1998

Bibliography

1. Showmen's League of America (2012) retrieved January 2013, photo from; http//www.showmensleague.org/showmens-rest

2. Wilbert (2013) retrieved February 2013photos, print from, http://www.wilbert.com/about/ history; http.//www.wilbert.com/about/timeline

3. Graceland Estate; memorial garden; Memphis, Tennessee self-photographed May 2009

4. News and Information about Geology (2005-2013), retrieved definition January 2013 from, http://www.geology.com/rocks/igneous-rock/

5. Memorials.com. Urns for cremation; veteran-bronze-headstones (2002-2013) retrieved March 2013 from, http://www.memorials.com

6. US Dept of Veterans Affairs (last updated April 15, 2013) VA National Cemetery Administration, retrieved January 2013 from, http//www.cem.va.gov/

7. All Faiths Cemetery; community mausoleum; New York(n.d.) retrieved February 2013, photograph from http//www.allfaithscemtery/mausoleums.htm

8. Bing Image Search (n.d.), retrieved February 2013 from, http://www.bing.com/images

9. http://www.bing.com/images/search?q=Chicago+shttp://www.bing.com/images/search?q=Chicago+skyline+over+cemeterwashingtony&qs=n&form; retrieved February 2013

10. Pontius Chapel Cemetery, Washington Township, Pickaway, Ohio (n.d.); retrieved February 2013 from http://Limestones.blogspot.com/2010/06/pontius-chapel-cemetery-washington.html

11. Photographs (n.d.), retrieved February 2013 from, http://headstones-tombstones-gravestones.com/carv-pieta;

12. Wreaths across America at Fort Logan National Cemetery of Colorado; retrieved January 2013 from, http://www.123rf.com

13. Cemetery scenes (n.d.), retrieved February 2013 from; http.//www.stay.com/Chicago/attractions/10791/bohemianna tionalcemetery

14. Ever Life Memorials (n.d.), retrieved April 2013 from; :http.//www.everlifememorials.com

15. WKClaw.com

16. Dignitymemorial.com

17. Medicalnewstoday.com

18. Arbutusfuneralservices.com

19. Loveliveson.com

20. Healingbrave.com

NOTES

NOTES